fast

thinkin

new

beginner

PEARSON EDUCATION LIMITED

Head Office:
Edinburgh Gate
Harlow CM20 2JE
Tel: +44 (0)1279 623623
Fax: +44 (0)1279 431059

London Office:
128 Long Acre
London WC2E 9AN
Tel: +44 (0)20 7447 2000
Fax: +44 (0)20 7240 5771
Website: www.business-minds.com

_____

First published in Great Britain in 2001

© Pearson Education Limited 2001

The right of Richard Templar to be identified as Author
of this Work has been asserted by him in accordance
with the Copyright, Designs and Patents Act 1988.

ISBN 0 273 65309 1

British Library Cataloguing in Publication Data
A CIP catalogue record for this book can be obtained from the British Library

10 9 8 7 6 5 4 3 2 1

Typeset by Pantek Arts Ltd, Maidstone, Kent.
Printed and bound in Great Britain by Ashford Colour Press, Hampshire.

The Publishers' policy is to use paper manufactured from sustainable forests.

fast thinking: new beginner

▶ **plan their first days**

▶ **brief them well**

▶ **integrate them smoothly**

by Richard Templar

contents

introduction 8

fast thinking gambles 12

1 your objective 14
What you want to achieve 14
How to achieve your aim 15
A monitoring system 16
Baggy trousers 16

2 before they start 18
What the new beginner is thinking 19
    Answering the questions 21
Company literature 22
Your attitude 23
The offer letter 25
Negotiating agreements 27
The contract 28
What they should bring 29
The company information pack 30
And what else have you got to do? 32
The letters 35

3 on the day 38

Fitting in 38

    Initiation rites and practical jokes 39

The buddy philosophy 39

    What does a buddy do? 41

    What a buddy doesn't do 44

What's next 45

    The environment 46

    The job 46

    The company 47

    The team 48

The pre-induction training week 49

Planning their day 51

    Encouragement 51

    Their arrival 53

    A priority engagement 53

    The first chat 56

Getting to know them better 57

    Things to avoid 58

It's a two-way process 60

Getting lost and getting tired 61

    Reassurance 62

Getting them started 63

    Doing something useful 64

Day two 66

4 different needs 70

People with disabilities 72
People with ethnic differences 73
Part-timers 74
Shift workers 74
Long-distance workers 74
Professionals 76
Women returners 76
Older workers 77
School leavers 77
Graduates 78
Managers 80
Expatriates 80
Transferees 80
Promotees 82
People returning to work after long
    unemployment 82
Ex-offenders 82
Temps 83
Job sharers 83
Home workers 84

5 follow-up procedures   86

Commitment   87

Plan   88

Action   89

Judging   90

new beginner in an hour   92

new beginner in 15 minutes   94

introduction

So, you've got a new beginner starting in your department tomorrow – a new team member. Brilliant. You sure could do with another pair of hands. But hang on a moment, isn't there something we're overlooking? Who is going to show this new team member their duties? Who is going to show them where the coffee machine is? Do we have any company systems to introduce this new person successfully to our working practices and conventions?

Yep, it's happened. You have less than 24 hours to learn, understand and put into place a full and complete induction programme. We're going to have to think at the speed of life. But don't panic. Help is at hand. *Fast Thinking: New Beginner* is your bible, your guide to the wonderful world of induction – the new beginner's programme for starting a new job. This book is about thinking fast and smart. This book cuts out the waffle and tells you what you really need to know about how to introduce a new team member successfully and efficiently, and how to make them truly feel at home.

Sure – it's better to have more time, and this book will tell you what to do with it when you *do* have it. But for now, what you need is the fast thinker's version. You want:

 tips for looking as if you know more than you really do

 shortcuts for doing as little preparation as you can (not because you are lazy but because you simply don't have the time)

 checklists to run through to make sure you've forgotten nothing

… and all presented clearly and simply. And short enough to read fast of course.

Ideally you would want longer and you would have started earlier – as far back as interview stage. But that's in an ideal world, and we're working in the real world where stuff hits fans at the last minute and there is never enough time to do things properly. All we can hope for is doing things well and looking good. You've only got a day and this is the time to wake up and smell the coffee – no time to drink it I'm afraid. If you're really up against the clock you may have only an hour to prepare, in which case there is a checklist at the back of the book to help you really get jet-propelled.

And if you've been given as little as 15 minutes (it does happen) there's a truly up-against-the-wall version to help you prepare faster than the speed of life.

So take the phone off the hook, take a deep breath and don't panic. It's all in here and this book will get you through the process of greeting and meeting, welcoming and installing a new beginner in your department in as little as 15 minutes if that's all you've got. Every minute you've got beyond that is a bonus. So stop thinking of your one whole day as too little and start thinking of it as a luxury. You've even got a little time to relax and have that coffee now.

NEW BEGINNER AT THE SPEED OF LIFE

This book is going to go through the five key stages of initiating a new beginner into a new job:

1. The first thing to do is identify your objective, so you know where you are going and the best way to get there.
2. Then we'll have a quick look at pre-employment preparation – what happens between interview and first day. Chances are, you won't have much time for any of this but at the very least it will be nice to know what should have happened so you can make sure it happens next time. You'll also need to know who is arriving, what job they are going to be doing, letting the rest of the team know, that sort of really basic stuff.
3. The next step is structuring a welcoming procedure so they feel right at home and you don't have to worry too much that they will get lost, bored or disenchanted with the job on their first day. And we'll have a quick look at training, including skills, knowledge and attitude, so your new beginner sees a long-term future ahead of them with you.
4. We will look at special need new beginners, such as women returning to work after having children, people with disabilities, ethnic minorities, older workers, part-timers, school leavers, graduates and executives.
5. And finally we'll look at follow-up procedures so you can keep an eye on your new beginner and not have them sink into the oblivion of the day-to-day running of your department.

So stop thinking of your one whole day as too little and start thinking of it as a luxury

fast thinking gambles

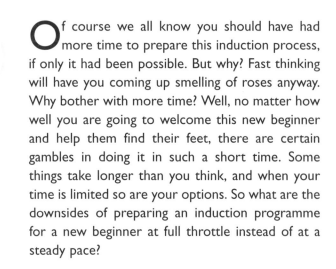

Of course we all know you should have had more time to prepare this induction process, if only it had been possible. But why? Fast thinking will have you coming up smelling of roses anyway. Why bother with more time? Well, no matter how well you are going to welcome this new beginner and help them find their feet, there are certain gambles in doing it in such a short time. Some things take longer than you think, and when your time is limited so are your options. So what are the downsides of preparing an induction programme for a new beginner at full throttle instead of at a steady pace?

> In your rush to get the person in, and show them where everything is and who everyone is and what everything is, you neglect a vital part of their training programme – such as how to actually do the job they've come to do.

- You are so rushed into this process that you choose someone completely unsuitable to show them round and they both go off and get lost.

- You are so busy that you fail to welcome them successfully and they leave before they ever had a chance to learn the job properly.

- You may pitch your induction procedure completely at the wrong level – instead of a school leaver working their very first day ever and needing to be shown where the toilets are, you instead have a senior member of management who is experienced and would like to know if your computer system is compatible with the ZX4000 system they were using in their last job and whether it speaks Cobalt Blue with 3D cadmium background Doppler effect. Gulp.

These are only a few of the risks and gambles – there are many more along the way – but you see why more time would have been helpful. But we can still do this and do it well if you follow this guide, which you've so cleverly bought and have open in front of you. This guide will turn a potentially fraught and embarrassing spectacle into a polished, efficient induction process that will leave your contemporaries gasping with admiration. But do try to leave more time, next time.

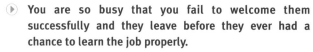
This guide will turn a potentially fraught and embarrassing spectacle into a polished, efficient induction process that will leave your contemporaries gasping with admiration

1 your objective

No matter how busy you are, no matter how short of time, there is always time to set an objective. Reason? Well, you wouldn't set off in your car with no destination in mind, would you? You wouldn't go and buy a train ticket to 'anywhere', would you? And you wouldn't ever embark on a business exercise without knowing:

- **what you want to achieve**
- **how to achieve your aim**
- **some form of monitoring system to check you have arrived at your goal.**

WHAT YOU WANT TO ACHIEVE

And what do you want to achieve? To get a new beginner settled in and off your hands as quickly and as painlessly as possible? No, not really. You want them to be welcomed, settle in, feel at home, understand their way around, know their duties, meet the other team members, have company procedures and policies explained to them – that sort of thing. So your aim might well be: *to induct the new beginner effectively and warmly*.

HOW TO ACHIEVE YOUR AIM

But how are we going to achieve that? I don't mean the detail but in general terms? Well, if money were no object we could give the new beginner a minder to follow them around for the first few weeks and explain everything. But in the real world – the one we live in – money *is* an object and we are limited in our resources. We have to induct the new beginner in a cost-effective way and still have them learn effectively and quickly. We can achieve this by inducting more than one new beginner at a time. And if we can't do this, we can have them follow a tailor-made package that will simplify things for them. We need to have induction systems in place *before* they arrive. So we can add to our objective by saying: *by following the guidelines already worked out*. (And don't worry if your company, for whatever reason, doesn't have an induction policy or guidelines for you to follow – we will look at setting that up a little later.)

We need to have induction systems in place *before* they arrive

A MONITORING SYSTEM

How will we know the new beginner has settled in well, is happy in their new employment and is working effectively and satisfactorily? We need some form of ongoing monitoring to make sure they don't get lost in the system. Our objective really should include something about this: *and to make sure their settling procedure is maintained satisfactorily.*

BAGGY TROUSERS

That's not too bad for a first go and it's only taken us a few minutes. I know the clock is ticking and you are

thinking smart

BUYING TIME

Allow yourself five minutes to think through your objective, and set a stop-watch. If you have only an hour before having to greet a new beginner then you may cut this down to three minutes. However, don't let it be any less than this. Tell yourself that, no matter how panicked you are, you will not use up less than your allocated five minutes. If you finish early, write it out again more neatly to pass the time. You will probably find five minutes is exactly the sort of time you do need though. Getting this bit right will save you plenty of time later on. This is the fundamental upon which everything else is built. Get it wrong or don't do it and you are building on shifting sands.

anxious to be off, panicking like anyone else would in this situation. But there really is no need. Once you have an objective, you can work through it in logical and easy steps. Management can be by the seat of your pants or by calm and rational fast thinking. One will get you baggy trousers and the other will get you the job done quickly and efficiently. You choose. So let's have a look at this objective:

> To induct the new beginner effectively and warmly by following the guidelines already worked out and to make sure their settling procedure is maintained satisfactorily.

Not bad. Sounds a bit formal. Perhaps we could make it a little less so:

> To settle the new beginner in a warm and efficient way, using the standard company procedures, and to make sure they continue to feel motivated, enthusiastic and happy in their work.

Not bad at all. Now we have a destination, something to measure our success by. We can confidently go out to greet the new beginner tomorrow knowing that we have a goal in sight.

Now you have your objective, write it down. This is your touchstone for the rest of the preparation you need to do. If any aspect of the induction process doesn't further this objective, then don't waste your time on it.

2 before they start

So, tomorrow the new beginner turns up and what have they come to expect of you? Yep, they will by now have formed an opinion of you and your company by what has already happened to them. Their image of you will have started the very instant they first saw the job advertised.

Now you may have had no control over the job advertising, but you will have been part of the interview and candidate-selection process, and it might even have been your final judgement that swung it in their favour. But the way you notified them that they'd got the job, and what they were to do after that and before actually turning up on the first day, is all part of their induction process. Probably without realizing it you have set the ball rolling, and let's hope you have done so effectively, warmly and well – see your objective. In case you're in any doubt, we will go over this pre-employment induction process so if you have fouled up or not done it as well as it might have been you can make

DON'T ASSUME

Just because they came for the interview and were successful at it doesn't mean you can relax and let things go. You mustn't assume they will actually turn up for that important first day. Anything you do now between the interview and their starting date can influence their decision as to whether or not to join your organization. Send them a letter *offering* them the job. Don't assume they will accept it. They may have gone for several interviews and been successful at all of them. Their decision will now be based on how you appear to be as a likely employer. Be friendly and welcoming in everything you send out.

notes and tighten up for next time. If you've only just bought this book, then a lot of this chapter will tell you what you should have done – it might not be too late. You can put together a welcome pack with most of the information in it. Make sure the person's name is on the front and that it looks professional and well presented.

WHAT THE NEW BEGINNER IS THINKING

Before the new beginner actually turn up to begin their new job with you, they will be asking themselves a lot of questions:

Probably without realizing it you have set the ball rolling, and let's hope you have done so effectively, warmly and well

- Will I fit in?
- What sort of rules will apply to me?
- Can I cope with this new job?
- Will I be happy working here?
- How nerve-wracking is my first day going to be?
- What sort of company is this?
- What are my long-term plans?

thinking smart

THE FIRST TWO WEEKS

Research has shown that people make their decision as to whether to stay or leave a company within the first two weeks of starting a new job – that's right, the *first two weeks*. And that's usually about the same length of time it takes for an induction process. It might just be that the two are linked. Get it right and they stay. Get it wrong and they leave. It really is as simple as that. And if you are going to spend the money in the first place training them, inducting them and employing them, then it makes economical and humanitarian sense to get it right. It costs you money to keep replacing staff and it simply isn't fair on them to induct them badly and make them suffer from poor management techniques. Not that that's you, as you are a fast and smart thinker – or you wouldn't be reading this.

And a whole lot more. Think back to whenever you've started a new job. There is trepidation, excitement and intrigue. You want to know how working for this company is going to affect you, and how your new work colleagues will take to you. These fears are only natural, but they can cloud the enjoyment of the first day. Your job, as a fast thinking and effective team leader, is to dispel these doubts before the person ever sets foot in the building.

Answering the questions

So what are you going to do about all these questions? Well, hopefully you will answer a lot of them and set the person's mind at rest. To do this, you will need to write to them before their first

 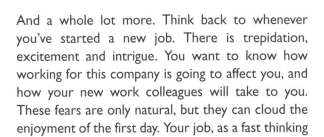

thinking smart

CONSISTENCY

You will have to make sure you are quite clear about what is *expected* of them as opposed to what is *accepted*. Make sure their first day is consistent with whatever literature you've sent out to them previously. There's not a lot of point in stressing that good timekeeping is a part of your requirements if they are immediately told by the rest of the team to ignore that as nothing happens if you're an hour late whenever you want to be. Make sure the rest of the team is in line before you introduce a new beginner.

day and send them basic literature about your team, their job, the company and the rules of behaviour expected of them.

COMPANY LITERATURE

The company literature you send out to your new beginner has a pretty major influence on the way they perceive your organization. When you are sending anything out to them, make sure it:

- ▶ **isn't too formal**
- ▶ **isn't worded in a terribly old-fashioned way**
- ▶ **carries positive images**
- ▶ **doesn't imply any discrimination**
- ▶ **doesn't carry any false promises**
- ▶ **makes the new beginner feel part of a 'family' rather than merely a small cog in a vast machine.**

thinking smart

DEAR SIR OR MADAM

Make sure any letters are addressed to the new beginner personally and not to 'Dear Sir or Madam'. When you suggest that they write back, instead of formal phrases such as 'Please reply to Mr Owen', use 'Please reply to Bob Owen'. This way you will have already gained an advantage before they even begin their induction process.

YOUR ATTITUDE

How you write to the new beginner is terribly important. They will get quite an insight into how you regard staff by the way you inform them that they have successfully got the job and what they have to do next. If your letters are pompous and full of unnecessarily formal phrases, they will see you as old-fashioned and out of touch. If your letters are short and brief to the point of rudeness, then that's how they will see you. Here are a couple of examples of what not to do:

Dear Miss Smith

It is with very great pleasure that I am happy to inform you that you have been selected as the successful candidate for the position of copywriter's assistant with MegaPlus and Company. We look forward to receiving you into our organization and would request that you commence your employment with us on Monday the 21st. If you would be so kind as to present yourself to the reception desk at 10 o'clock promptly, you will be instructed as to your duties and responsibilities.

We take this opportunity to enclose a formal contract, which you should sign and return to Mr Partridge in personnel by the 13th of this month.

We hope your employment with us will be mutually beneficial.

Your faithfully

Mr Owen, Senior Team Leader

> Dear Miss Smith
> You got the job. Be here on the 21st at 10 o'clock. Enclosed contract. Please sign and return to personnel by the 13th. Good luck.
> Mr Owen, Senior Team Leader

Both of these leave the new beginner feeling somewhat less impressed than they may have been. How about:

> Dear Barbara
> Congratulations. We are happy that you have been successfully chosen for the job as copywriter's assistant. Could you come in on the 21st around 9 o'clock? And please let reception know when you are here as I would like to welcome you in person.
>
> You will find enclosed a contract of employment. Please have a good read of it and if there is anything you don't understand feel free to give Tony Partridge in personnel a ring on extension 2341. He will be only too happy to explain anything you need him to. Once you are happy with the contract could you let us have it back – preferably by the 13th please.
>
> I look forward to seeing you on the 21st and also enclose a company information pack for you to have a look at. Any questions, give me a ring on extension 2345.
> Regards
> Bob Owen, Senior Team Leader

There, that should make them feel encouraged, wanted and respected.

- 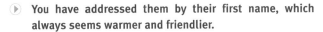 You have addressed them by their first name, which always seems warmer and friendlier.

- You have *asked* them to come in on the 21st rather than telling them, but you have also repeated the date later so they know they don't really have a lot of choice. Even so, you have given them a get-out if they really can't make that day.

- You have signalled that 'Bob' and 'Tony' are OK names to use, rather than Mr this and Mrs that.

- You have been friendly and signalled warmth – the use of 'please' and 'happy'.

- You have given them vital information if they don't understand something – extension numbers and who to ring.

- You have indicated that you don't expect them to understand everything right from the word go and that you will be forgiving and understanding if they need to know anything.

- You have indicated that you genuinely look forward to meeting them and welcoming them into your company.

THE OFFER LETTER

Good. Now what else? Quickly, as the clock is ticking and tomorrow is looming. Well, we need to have a quick look at what else you should have sent out prior to this new beginner joining you. Here's a checklist:

You have addressed them by their first name, which always seems warmer and friendlier

- ▶ the starting salary/wages and any other financial packages on offer

- ▶ the job being filled, with a job title, objective and brief description of duties and responsibilities

- ▶ the starting date, where to report and at what time – include also where to park or nearest Tube station

- ▶ how they are to be paid – monthly/weekly, by direct transfer/in cash, on a Thursday/last day of the month

- ▶ the grade of the job and what that means – such as Technician grade 4, salary band £x to £x

- ▶ where they are to work – they may have been interviewed at your Slough office but are actually working in the admin block at Maidenhead

- ▶ basic terms and conditions – sick pay, maternity leave, pension plans, holidays, hours of work, breaks, meals, accrued holiday pay entitlements, the probationary period

- ▶ any salary progressions

- ▶ any company discipline procedures (see *Fast Thinking: Discipline*)

- ▶ details of any relocation packages on offer

- ▶ the name of their direct supervisor

- ▶ who to report to on their first day

- ▶ the size of the team they will be joining, and a rough guide to who they will be working with – 'There are 20 of us here in the finance office and the average age is 30, so you should feel at home'

- **any special factors, such as dress standards, special clothing to be worn, e.g. hairnets, flat shoes, white overalls. Indicate where this special clothing can be obtained from, and who is paying.**

You should also make sure that it is quite clear whether or not the job offer is subject to you obtaining satisfactory references and/or medical checks. If they do have to have a medical check, you will have to explain:

- **where**
- **who is paying (the company of course)**
- **what the medical is for – for example colour blindness if you are employing a paint chart mixer.**

NEGOTIATING AGREEMENTS

Obviously, a lot of the previously mentioned job offer details are not negotiable. But what if they are? Well, you should have cleared up a lot of things at interview stage. But make sure they know that if there is anything that they really are not happy about they can give you a ring, and that you are happy to discuss – and thus negotiate – anything with them.

But make sure they know that if there is anything that they really are not happy about they can give you a ring

IT AIN'T OVER UNTIL ...

... they walk through the door on their first day – and even then it is still a trial period. For them of course. They have the right to walk out again. And before they do walk in, they have the right to not take you up on your wonderful job offer. They may change their mind, decide to tell you to stick it, be upset by something you send out, get a better offer, decide to throw it all in and go round the world. You simply don't know, so don't take chances. You obviously want them or you wouldn't have advertised the job, been through the selection process, held interviews, made a decision and offered them the job. Don't throw it all away at the last minute by sounding unfriendly or boring or old-fashioned.

THE CONTRACT

You don't legally have to offer an employee a written contract until they have been with you for 13 weeks. But the second they start, you have an unwritten one so you might as well go the whole hog and do the honourable thing and offer the contract before they begin the new job. We can't cover the scope of the legal niceties of the written employment contract in this book, but you should make sure that you have included:

- ▶ **the name of the employer**
- ▶ **the name of the employee**
- ▶ **the periods of notice on either side (you need to check the statutory minimum)**
- ▶ **the probationary period and how it can be extended (or not) if the work isn't quite up to standard**
- ▶ **hours of work**
- ▶ **salary**
- ▶ **starting date**
- ▶ **what the job entails**
- ▶ **how performance is judged.**

Remember that this is a legally binding document and must be prepared professionally.

WHAT THEY SHOULD BRING

Phew. Bet there is a lot more here than you realized. And we haven't finished yet. You should have told them what to bring with them tomorrow. Haven't? Might need to give them a ring now and tell them to bring:

- ▶ **P45 and National Insurance number**
- ▶ **bank account details, if that's how you pay their salary**
- ▶ **certificates of qualifications you might need to see**

Don't throw it all away at the last minute by sounding unfriendly or boring or old-fashioned

- ▶ any work permits required

- ▶ driving licence, if required

- ▶ birth certificate, if required

- ▶ their sandwiches (no joke this – if you don't provide lunch or there isn't a canteen, make sure they know)

- ▶ any dates they can't work for some reason, such as a previously booked holiday

- ▶ any uniform or special clothing – you should have sorted this out already, but it helps to remind them

- ▶ special tools of the trade – again, they may well know this, but a reminder saves any embarrassment

- ▶ any forms that needed signing and returning, such as acceptance letter, contract, personnel record card

- ▶ any licence they may need to carry out their employment.

THE COMPANY INFORMATION PACK

Good. Now we're moving along. And what did you send out that wasn't part of their direct employment details? Why, the company information pack of course. You did, didn't you? Of course you did, but just to make sure yours was bang up to date and really useful, here is a quick checklist of what should have gone out. If you forget to send it, make sure you have one to hand the new beginner first thing tomorrow morning:

thinking smart

NOT FIRST THING

If the rest of your team members normally start work at 9 o'clock, then don't schedule a new beginner to start at this time. They will get lost in the crowds and feel intimidated. Get them to start a little later – say 10 o'clock. This also gives you a chance to clear your desk of anything urgent, sort out any pressing problems, have a cup of coffee, make sure the team is in place and working effectively, and generally compose yourself.

Have a cup of coffee, make sure the team is in place and working effectively, and generally compose yourself

This is what the company information pack should contain in an ideal world:

- ▶ **a letter from the company chairman or managing director welcoming them**

- ▶ **a chart explaining the hierarchy of the organization, showing job titles and names**

- ▶ **a welcome letter from any trade union or staff association they can join**

- ▶ **any literature on customer care**

- ▶ **any political, religious or philosophical ideology the company may have**

- ▶ **company history, size and subsidiaries**

- ▶ **the company mission statement**

- ▸ any sales literature that is relevant

- ▸ financial reports and/or last annual report (probably included only for fairly senior staff)

- ▸ details of any social clubs or activities the new beginner can be part of.

AND WHAT ELSE HAVE YOU GOT TO DO?

Bet you're wishing you'd never taken on this new beginner now. Don't despair. We're almost through

thinking smart

THE TOUR

It is often considered a useful exercise to offer the new beginner a tour round the place of work before they start. About a week in advance is the right sort of time, as they then don't forget everything before starting. This tour gives them an idea of what they are to expect, and will also outline any future problems they may have before they crop up – 'Oh, I didn't realize you all sat on high stools like that at the work benches; I couldn't possibly sit up there as I'm frightened of heights,' or 'But you all smoke and I'm a non-smoker; what am I to do?'

Giving them a quick tour is a friendly thing to do, and it gives the rest of the team a chance to get to know them – even if only slightly – so that when they start they will know what to expect.

the pre-employment stuff, and then we can get on to the really exciting briefing – the day itself. I know time is limited and there is so much to take in, but you are thinking fast, thinking smart and you can do it.

What is left to do? Well, here is a quick checklist. Oh no, not another one! Yep, but would you rather have to wade through pages of bumf to extract the key points yourself? I thought not. Here's the essence without the waffle:

- ▶ **Make sure you have provided adequate stationery and equipment for the new beginner.**

- ▶ **Make sure that they have been allocated a workspace/ desk, and that it is suitably clean and fresh for their arrival.**

thinking smart

GO THAT LITTLE BIT FURTHER

You might like to provide some fresh flowers or a new potted plant if you really want to impress. Or how about a new coffee mug? Or a smart new blotter and telephone pad? A new set of pens/pencils? Anything that is relatively inexpensive could help them feel welcomed, and is a great personal touch without costing the earth. Be consistent, though – and provide an extra treat for all new beginners or none at all.

Be consistent, though – and provide an extra treat for all new beginners or none at all

- ▶ Make sure that they have any keys and security passes necessary.

- ▶ Door nameplates and business cards should have been ordered if they are needed (make sure you've used the name and personal title that *they* want, for example their preference for Ms Julia Newton rather than J. Newton).

- ▶ Other staff and colleagues should have been briefed about their arrival.

- ▶ Gate security and reception staff should have been notified of their arrival, along with their name, job title and where they should go.

- ▶ Make sure that you know exactly what you are going to do with this new beginner on their first day and during their first few weeks.

- ▶ Ensure you have scheduled time in to greet them and be part of the induction process.

- ▶ Any training that you think necessary should have been arranged, places on courses booked, and supervisory staff informed.

- ▶ The post room and switchboard should have been notified of the new beginner.

- ▶ The new beginner should have been allocated an extension number if necessary.

- ▶ Is there any information from the previous job holder that might prove useful you could supply?

- ▶ Have they been allocated a locker if required, and has it been cleaned out after the previous occupant?

- ▶ **Do they need allocating a computer password? Has this been done?**

- ▶ **Are you ready? Do you need a refresher course on training new starters? (Of course not, you've got this book.) Do you know all the terms and conditions applicable to a new beginner, and are you totally familiar with company induction policy and practice?**

- ▶ **Have personnel been informed and do they have all the right information?**

There, that will do for now. We have almost finished the pre-employment stages. The actual day – tomorrow – should seem like a doddle compared to all the stuff you have to do in advance.

THE LETTERS

We looked earlier at the letter you send out telling the new beginner that they have been successful in their interview and at this stage you are making them a formal job offer. That's the first letter.

They should reply, accepting – hopefully – your kind and generous offer.

Now you have to send out the welcoming letter. This should contain the joining instructions. In other words:

- ▶ details of what they need to bring with them
- ▶ where and when to start
- ▶ whom to report to
- ▶ details of the induction period with relevant training
- ▶ the welcome pack.

Good. That's the new beginner written to. Now you have to formally tell personnel. You will need to supply details, such as:

- ▶ The person's name, address, National Insurance number and/or P45.
- ▶ Personal details, such as date of birth, sex, telephone number, nationality, and medical information.
- ▶ Details of the work itself, including references, proof of qualifications, pay-roll number, union number, bank account details, pension scheme details, previous occupation, holiday entitlement, details of the contract issued and signed, department, details of work permit, if required.

And now you've finished. Well done. You now have a pretty comprehensive knowledge of what's required of you before the new beginner actually turns up tomorrow. Do go back over the checklists quickly and just make sure you haven't forgotten anything.

for next time

Check the lists regularly if you take on lots of new beginners or are unfamiliar with the protocol.

Keep records of everything you do so you have some form of history to refer back to.

Make sure that everyone on the team understands what is expected and required of them – they can make or break a new beginner's morale quicker than anything you can do to welcome them. If you feel it would help, train your team in how to help newcomers to settle in.

Don't use pre-prepared letters to offer a new beginner a job or to welcome them. Make each letter personal and friendly. There is nothing worse than feeling you, as a new beginner, are a tiny part of some vast, faceless organization before you've even started. Make your letters human.

There is nothing worse than feeling you, as a new beginner, are a tiny part of some vast, faceless organization before you've even started

3 on the day

So the big day has dawned and you are about to welcome the new beginner. You have done everything in your power already, by following all the checklists in the previous chapter, to make sure this is a successful and enjoyable day for them.

All you've got to do now is check that you know everything they will need to know about. Their first day is going to be pretty nerve-wracking, and anything you can do to reassure them and make them feel confident and happy will go a long way to making sure that they stay and that their induction process is effective.

FITTING IN

Some new beginners seem to fit in right away; they are confident and settle in easily. Others take longer and need more reassurance.

How the new beginner fits in with the rest of the team is very important. Obviously there will be a certain amount of caution on everyone's side as the old team make way for a new member. Judgements will be made if they are taking someone else's post, especially if the one who left was well liked and popular. Naturally, there will be a certain desire on the part of the old team to want the new beginner to shape up quickly and fit it.

Initiation rites and practical jokes

In some institutions there might well be practical jokes played on the new beginner or even more serious 'initiation rites' performed. If the job entails any danger where team members have to trust and rely on each other for their very lives – such as the fire brigade, the army or mountain rescue teams – these initiation rites can be extreme to say the least. How you view these pranks or rites is entirely up to you, but there does seem to be some evidence that a certain amount of 'bonding' may be necessary for the old team to accept the new team member. Bear in mind that when the new beginner is no longer seen as a threat they will have successfully passed their team's admittance programme – however unofficial this is. If the jokes continue too long, or are too harsh or personal, the new beginner will simply leave. You need to monitor the situation without being seen to interfere or discriminate.

THE BUDDY PHILOSOPHY

Many companies subscribe to the view that appointing each new beginner a 'buddy' will be beneficial. This system has been found to be extremely helpful to the new beginner and allows them to be inducted faster and more effectively. The buddy shows them the ropes and is on hand to answer any questions the new beginner will have – and there will be a lot of them. If you don't like the American term, you can call them a 'companion', a 'sponsor', a 'chum' or a 'starter's friend'. It's entirely up to you, but I shall continue to call them buddies.

The buddy performs many vital roles to enable the new beginner to settle in quickly. There are some ground rules, such as:

- The buddy should be a similar age to the new beginner.

- The buddy should be of a roughly equal status, and certainly never junior.

- They should have some things in common if possible, e.g. they both live in the same area of town, they both share martial arts as a hobby, they both drive 2CVs – that sort of thing.

- The buddy should also be relatively new to the company as well – but obviously not another new beginner – as they will still have a fresh memory of the rules and procedures.

- It should only be a temporary arrangement.

- The buddy should be a willing party to this and not press ganged into it.

- The buddy should be an accepted member of the team, not an outsider or an unpopular member of the team.

- The buddy should have a confident personality and be outgoing and friendly.

If you find someone who has all these qualities and requirements, let me know and I'll employ them as a buddy to my new beginners. Obviously this is a wish list – just make sure your buddy fulfils as many as possible.

What does a buddy do?

OK, we've established that choosing a buddy needs some thought, but what do you do with a buddy now you've got one?

thinking smart

CLOSING-DOWN PROCEDURE

Make sure the new beginner knows what to do at the end of the day. This might be as mundane as making sure all the windows are shut, but it might also involve training in setting burglar alarms, signing out at reception, collecting a pager, taking work home, signing for a laptop, reporting to a supervisor or logging off a computer terminal. Whatever your closing-down procedure is, make sure the new beginner is well versed in it and doesn't feel confused at the end of the day.

Well, having a buddy is very useful to the new beginner, and to you as well. From the buddy, you can get useful information about how the new beginner is settling in, how they seem to fit in with the rest of the team, and any problems they may be having. All you have to do is trust the buddy to be your eyes and ears, and to report back to you at the end of the first day and the end of the first week.

The buddy should be responsible for:

- showing the new beginner where to hang their coat
- showing them where and when to go for lunch
- showing them where things are
- introducing them individually to the rest of the team

thinking smart

INTRODUCE THE BUDDY BEFOREHAND

In an ideal world you would appoint the buddy long before the new beginner starts, and then get the buddy to make contact with them prior to their start day. This gives the new beginner a familiar face to help them feel at home on their first day. If you give new beginners a tour, then you could introduce the buddy at the same time. The buddy could even be the one to give the tour.

- letting the new beginner know about rules – both standard and unwritten ones

- demonstrating how to log on to computers, operate security systems, and operate equipment such as photocopiers, telephones, fax machines and shredders.

- explaining how the breaks work, what they do about the post, and basic on-the-job instruction

The buddy basically takes the pressure off you. Make sure you tell the buddy what you expect of them and how they should report back to you. You need a sort of mini buddy induction training programme.

thinking smart

MANNING THE LUNCHTIME PHONES

A lot of offices insist that when everyone goes off to lunch someone remains behind to answer the phone. The new beginner should be immune from this chore for the first month. It is impolite not to make sure they get included in lunch and that way they also get to know the rest of the team better and socially. In any case, there is simply no point leaving them to staff the phones as they won't have a clue what they should be saying or doing, or who anyone is.

If you give new beginners a tour, then you could introduce the buddy at the same time. The buddy could even be the one to give the tour

What a buddy doesn't do

The buddy shouldn't be the one to greet the new beginner. That's down to you. It is polite, courteous and friendly for the team leader to be the one to go to reception – or wherever the new beginner has to report to on their first day – and shake hands, welcome them warmly and escort them to their place of work. You can take them into your office to begin with and give them a chat about what you expect of them, but they probably just need to be handed over to their buddy to ease their shaking nerves.

The buddy shouldn't be responsible for collecting their personal details, their personnel records, their work permit or anything of that nature. Again, that's your job. You can take anything like that off them when you greet them at reception.

thinking smart

REQUISITIONING STORES

Make sure the new beginner knows how to get hold of the stuff they need to do their job properly. This might be paper, ink, toner cartridges, a laptop, pads, pens, staples, post-it notes, in-trays – whatever. There should be a system for requisitioning stores and they should stick to it – and so should the rest of the team.

The buddy doesn't introduce the new beginner to the whole team. You do that. Then you hand over to the buddy, and they do the rest of the introductions individually without you being there. If you are there, it will only serve to make it all terribly formal and stilted. You can say, 'Hi, team, this is Julia. She's starting with us today [as you told them all last week] as the new graphic designer. Andy is going to be her buddy for the next week or two. I'll let him show her where everything is, and then you can meet her and have a chat once she's hung up her coat and had a cup of coffee.' Then leave for a while. You can drop back a little later on to check her progress. After she has settled in a bit, the buddy can introduce her individually to the rest of the team, but maybe only the ones she needs to work with initially as too many new faces can be daunting – you never remember all the names and you forget which ones you need to know.

What's next?

So the buddy has taken over a major part of your role, and you can now go back to the office, put your feet up and relax. Your job is done and the new beginner is settled in. In your dreams. There's still a lot for you to do. Time is marching on and we

So the buddy has taken over a major part of your role, and you can now go back to the office, put your feet up and relax

must work at the speed of life if we are to cover everything before tomorrow and the reality of your new beginner.

You need a plan of action – a sort of map of the new beginner's needs. We'll cover this as quickly as possible by using checklists without the waffle. You need to be aware that the new beginner needs to know:

The environment

- ▸ surroundings
- ▸ the way round the building
- ▸ travel arrangements
- ▸ where and what the facilities are
- ▸ health and safety procedures
- ▸ fire drills
- ▸ security
- ▸ what they have to do about maintenance and repairs.

The job

- ▸ what it entails
- ▸ what the job does not include
- ▸ what standards you expect
- ▸ what to do if things go wrong

- ▶ their limits of authority
- ▶ how their work standards will be measured
- ▶ what information they will need
- ▶ what equipment they have at their disposal
- ▶ the challenge of the job
- ▶ availability of information and feedback
- ▶ methods of communication
- ▶ any special jargon or language they need to know.

The company

- ▶ what it does
- ▶ its suppliers and customers
- ▶ its mission statement
- ▶ its subsidiaries

thinking smart

MAKE THEM FEEL SPECIAL

If your new beginner has to be given an in-tray, for example, make sure it is a new one and not one covered in the last employee's stickers, graffiti and used chewing gum. Make your new beginner feel special by making them feel as if they deserve the best. This is a quick and inexpensive way to get them feeling good about you and the company.

- its parent company
- the security it offers
- its history and future
- the facilities it offers its employees.

The team

- the hierarchy
- subordinates
- peers
- supervisors
- other colleagues
- social contacts
- what is expected of them in terms of discriminatory policies
- group dynamics
- expectations of the team
- how the team meshes together
- who they have to work with.

Phew. That's a lot, and obviously you aren't going to give it all to them on their first day. You have to break it down into manageable chunks. And here, your buddy can become very useful. A lot of the above points can be introduced successfully over the first few weeks by the buddy. Your job is to make sure the buddy helps the new beginner learn the important things first, and that they are not overloading the new beginner with too much information. Your new beginner may well want to know all about the company, but their first concern undoubtedly will be with their actual job itself – what they have to do to earn their crust.

THE PRE-INDUCTION TRAINING WEEK

Some companies take the new beginner off for a week's training before their first day in the workplace. This can be successful as it teaches them what they are supposed to be doing, but a lot of new beginners find this very stressful as it invariably takes them away from home, often

thinking smart

AT THE END OF THE FIRST DAY

Make sure the new beginner reports to you at the end of the day for a final round-up of any problems – this should be a very quick chat as they will be anxious to get off home – and for you to monitor how they've done and how they feel about their first day. Make sure the buddy also reports back to you at the end of the first day and gives you a progress report.

Your new beginner may well want to know all about the company, but their first concern undoubtedly will be with their actual job itself

isolates them in a hotel overnight (or nights), and sometimes makes them feel that whatever they are being shown will be completely divorced from the reality of what actually goes on in the workplace.

On-the-job training may be more beneficial in the long run. But whatever you decide, make sure the tone of the first day – and weeks – is totally positive. Let them arrive later than the rest of the team and let them leave earlier. Praise them on settling in so well and so quickly. Try to remember your own first day and be aware that they have too much information to absorb, too many faces and names to remember, and too many new experiences to take it all in. They will be tired and unsettled. Let them go home without calling them in for a lengthy review. Don't ask, 'So, what do you think of us after your first day?' This leaves them stumped for an answer – if they think little of you they can't really say it, and if they thought a lot they'll think they sound toadying if they say so.

Nor should you say things like, 'So, that was quite a quiet day – but you just wait until next week, that's when we get really busy!' You'll just discourage them and make them feel inadequate.

But we're jumping the gun here. They haven't even started and already we're sending them home after their first day. Still it pays to be prepared.

FURTHER READING

If you have any useful books on any aspect of their new job, it might be worthwhile lending them to the new beginner at the end of their first day. It will make them feel as if you care (of course you do, but you must also be seen to do so) and it gives them something to take home and read while they are relaxing in the bath after their first long, hard day – or short, easy one, depending on which school of induction you subscribe to.

PLANNING THEIR DAY

For an inexperienced new beginner, you might be best leaving the day to shape itself. Let the buddy set the tone and pace. For more experienced staff, you need a timetable to keep them busy, get them involved and show them you trust their judgement and coping skills. You may need to discuss with them an agenda in case they just want to get on with it, meet the rest of the team first, have some training, have a tour of the building – whatever they feel they need to settle in quickly and effectively.

Encouragement

Make sure you encourage the new beginner during the day. Encourage them to ask questions by making sure they don't feel stupid or embarrassed. They will forget a lot and have to ask the same questions several times to become fully conversant with everything. Encourage them by letting them know that they are doing well and that no one expects too much of them on their first day. Encourage them to use their initiative and to set the pace themselves. Encourage them to get on with something useful if that's what they feel they need to do. If they don't do any actual work, they may go home feeling like a spare part. Obviously you have to set realistic goals for them to achieve, but you can get them helping other team members, which encourages social contact. Encourage them

thinking smart

GOING WITH THE CROWD

If everyone disappears to the pub at lunchtime, make sure the new beginner doesn't feel they have to. They may not be able to afford it. They may not want a drink. They may need a bit of peace and quiet. They may feel intimidated by refusing, so make sure they have an easy get-out if they want and don't get press-ganged into going.

If they do go, monitor their alcohol consumption and make sure they don't drink too much to cover up any nerves they may have.

to feel free to wander about a bit so they can get their bearings rather than sitting at their desk or workplace all day long. Finally, encourage them to come to you with any problems to do with work or settling in.

Their arrival

There really is only one person who should greet the new beginner at reception – and that's you, as we've already seen. But the receptionist should certainly make them feel welcome. You will have informed reception that they are arriving – at what time, their name and department, and all that – so all reception staff have to do is invite them to wait and inform you.

A priority engagement

As you have put this in your diary, consider it an important priority engagement. There simply is no reason to be delayed or late unless the office is on fire. If it was a client booked in, you'd make pretty damn sure you were on time, so do the same for your new beginner. It sets the tone for politeness and respect that should hopefully last their entire working life with you.

If, for reasons of layout, you can't get to reception to greet them, it is permissible to have

If everyone disappears to the pub at lunchtime, make sure the new beginner doesn't feel they have to

someone show them to where you are. But they must never be told where to go and set off alone. That is simply unforgivable and potentially frightening for them if they get lost.

Make sure you remember who they are and why they are there. Once you've greeted them warmly, you might like to hand them over to personnel if that is appropriate. Personnel can then take over the completion of their initial documentation. The sort of things they will need to know are:

thinking smart

DON'T SPOIL THEIR FIRST DAY

Don't allow the person's first day to be spoilt by unintentionally making a gaffe such as parking in the MD's car parking space, hanging their coat on someone else's peg, sitting in the wrong chair at the wrong desk, using someone else's favourite coffee mug, not bringing their lunch when they should have, getting lost, getting told off for using the wrong entrance, inadvertently addressing someone by the wrong name or title and being made to feel small for doing so, having to ask to use the lavatory, having to ask the same questions over and over again and being made to feel stupid for doing so, forgetting something vital such as their P45, or just being late. Be kind and fairly forgiving on their first day. It will pay in the long run if their initial impression is one of tolerance and consideration.

- national Insurance number, P45 details and bank/ building society numbers
- proof of qualifications, driving licence and birth certificate
- details of next of kin, and name and address of doctor
- full name and address
- pension details.

We have already covered all of these, with the exception of next of kin details, but these are only for use in an emergency and hopefully won't be needed.

thinking smart

FALSE EXPECTATIONS

No one can start a new job and do well immediately without supervision, training, encouragement and support. Fail to give any of these and they will flounder. Give them all and they will reward you with a job well done. Their productivity goes up in direct relation to the amount of help they get. Leave them alone to make a mess of things and your investment will not pay off. Your job does not stop when they start – it begins. Don't expect them to do well immediately. They won't. They are only human.

The first chat

Before you move the person along to meet their buddy, you need to have a little chat with them. You can do this in a very informal way over a cup of coffee. The important thing is to make them feel welcome, relaxed and 'at home'. Put them at their ease and explain that you want to have a chat to make sure they:

- ▶ understand the job that they have been employed to do

- ▶ are fully aware of what their contract means

- ▶ know how and when they will be paid – and how much of course

- ▶ understand why certain policies are in force

- ▶ know the hierarchy (not in too much detail at this stage)

- ▶ have, and will read, their copy of the employee handbook

- ▶ have been given instructions on using their company car (if applicable)

- ▶ understand rules about dress codes, conduct, house styles, discipline procedures and equal opportunities

- ▶ understand any company instructions about dealing with the public, press or any complaint procedures.

You must avoid the 'here's a load of bumf' technique, in which you hand them armfuls of papers and pat them on the head before sending them on their very confused way. Take your time and go through things with them. You don't have to go through everything in a lot of detail, just enough so that they know what it is you are giving them – or telling them – and so that they will be able to find any document again and know what it refers to and why.

GETTING TO KNOW THEM BETTER

This shouldn't take too long at all – probably about 15 minutes. You can even get personnel to deal with a lot of this if you prefer. Once all the documentation is out of the way you can get to know the new beginner better. Give them an idea of what they can expect today and for the next week or two. Explain about the buddy system and how it works. Find out how they got there this morning and what the journey was like. Ask about

thinking smart

INVESTING TIME

I know time is valuable but so too is your new beginner. The more time you invest in them, the better they will settle in. There is no short cut to spending time with them. It pays dividends later.

their personal preferences for music, food or whatever to establish some rapport and bonding.

Things to avoid

- **intimidating them**
- **overloading them with information**
- **patronizing them**
- **hurrying them**
- **making them feel you are really too busy to deal with them**
- **forgetting their name or what they are there for**
- **dismissing them too quickly and handing them over to someone else to get rid of them**

thinking smart

CHOOSING THE BUDDY

Make sure you choose a buddy who toes the party line. If you all take 15 minutes for a tea break mid-morning, then make sure this information is conveyed correctly by the buddy, not, 'Oh, and we are supposed to take 15 minutes but we all stretch that out to half an hour.'

Obviously the buddy will convey any unwritten rules so you might need to tighten the team up a bit if they have got lax before the new beginner latches on to bad habits.

- being irritated at having to repeat yourself because they didn't understand you the first time
- telling them how much money you've invested in them
- telling them how good their predecessor was
- failing to reassure them or make them feel welcomed.

I'm sure you won't do any of these but it is always best to know which ones you are likely to do – and thus be on the lookout for them. We are human

thinking smart

EMERGENCIES AND SAFETY

Have you briefed the new beginner in all relevant emergency and safety procedures? These include bomb scares, fire drill, being trapped in the lift, building evacuation, first aid (including first-aid points and first-aiders), sickness at work (including company doctor if you have one), accidents, health and safety risks (dangerous substances, food contamination, no-smoking zones, keeping passageways clear, keeping fire exits clear), protective clothing (if relevant), electrocution, carcinogenic substances (photocopier toner, paints, acetates, inks), radiation hazards, and repetitive strain injury (RSI). There may be others not listed here but relevant to your business. Walk around your work area and notice anything that may need pointing out to a new beginner unfamiliar with your working practices.

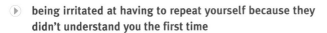

Walk around your work area and notice anything that may need pointing out to a new beginner unfamiliar with your working practices after all, and prone to being too busy or too stressed to do things properly. Obviously not you, as you have taken the time and trouble to get it right by buying this book. Score extra brownie points for diligence and smart thinking. Well done.

It's a two-way process

So, you are on your best behaviour and doing it all right. But what about them? Are they reading this? Probably not. Which means they won't be following an up-to-date business programme written specifically to put them at their ease. Instead they are going to be pretty nervous and likely to make appalling gaffes. They are quite likely to turn up at the wrong time, in the wrong place, and on the wrong day. And this isn't just school leavers. Executives, graduates and senior managers have been known to go to pieces on the first day in a new job and get it all wrong. It isn't just nerves about meeting new people. They're likely to be worrying about whether or not they can do the job, especially if this is a promotion. Different people worry about different things. The younger they are the more they tend to worry about fitting in, making friends and being accepted, whereas older people tend to worry about the responsibilities of the job.

thinking smart

THE OFFICE GRAPEVINE

Like it or not, there is one. There always is. And it can be quite an influence on how the new beginner views your organization. If the office grapevine is abuzz with rumours of take-overs, redundancies, sackings and relocations, they'll feel unsettled and nervous. It's your job as team leader to know what the latest gossip is – and it's also your job to make sure it stops. Gossip is the result of poorly communicated information and, as a smart thinker, you regularly hold team briefings to stop this sort of nonsense. You can warn the new beginner if rumours are flying around and tell them that if they don't hear it from you they can ignore it. You are the official line. Brief your team that they too should give the official line to new beginners.

GETTING LOST AND GETTING TIRED

So your job is to reassure all these different people with their different worries that they are all unfounded and that everything is going to be fine for them. They will all worry about getting lost, being taken seriously, being liked, getting enough information to do the job and not being left floundering, satisfying superiors sufficiently to stay in the job and finish the trial period and avoiding mistakes. They are on their toes and highly

So your job is to reassure all these different people with their different worries that they are all unfounded and that everything is going to be fine for them

nervous, which makes it more likely that they will make mistakes. They will also get tired. Tiredness is a natural way for the body to handle stress such as a first day. Give them lots of breaks and a chance to sit down as frequently as possible.

Reassurance

You will also need to reassure them about all the other worries. Show them charts of the company

thinking smart

THE OFFICE AFFAIR

It happens from time to time. And what do you say to the new beginner? If you say nothing, they risk putting their foot in it. If you say anything, you risk breaking confidences, alienating staff, spreading rumours that may not be as true as you think – and generally putting yourself in the firing line. The smart thing to do is to pitch your presentation in the middle by saying something like, 'Oh, and you may hear some rumours about Alice in your department and Charlie in production. I've no idea whether they're true or not but I thought you should know.' This way you've left yourself in the clear if it's not true – although you know full well it is – and you've given them some warning so they don't say anything negative about Charlie without realizing. Obviously this applies only to people they are working with directly. It is also worth pointing out who is married to whom as a similar precaution.

structure and point out exactly where they fit in. If you are their immediate supervisor or manager or team leader, you will need to go through with them their exact duties and what is expected of them. If you are at one remove from them, you can hand this over to their immediate supervisor.

GETTING THEM STARTED

A lot of what we have talked about up to now has been the admin and reassurance part of the package. But there is another side to all this. They are here to do a job of work. This is their first day. The best thing you could do for them is to get them to do some meaningful work.

thinking smart

WHAT IF SOMETHING GOES WRONG?

Does your new beginner know what to do if equipment fails? Is there a proscribed way of getting repairs done, calling an engineer, or notifying maintenance? There should be, and everyone should tackle the problem in the same way. Repairs should be left to qualified professionals, not handled by team members. Even if Billy from despatch knows exactly where to hit the photocopier to get it to work, it shouldn't be encouraged. Get it fixed properly by the proper person and make sure the new beginner knows the procedure.

HANDLING A POTENTIALLY DIFFICULT SITUATION

What if the job they've successfully applied for and got was also applied for by someone they have to work with closely? What are you going to do about this potentially difficult situation? Do you tell the new beginner? Evidence suggests that telling them is the smart thing to do. If the team member who applied for the job was considered too junior or not right for the promotion, then your new beginner won't have too much of a problem once they convince the team member of their suitability. If the team member is of equal status, then the new beginner will have to find ways to work with them without upsetting them – no boasting, bragging, or rubbing salt into wounds. It has to be handled diplomatically, which is why the new beginner always needs to know.

Doing something useful

New beginners need to do something useful on their first day if they are to feel worthwhile and that they have achieved something. Giving them something real to do will make them feel a part of the team much quicker than if you leave them to read through company literature.

Your aim should be to stop them getting bored, and finding real work for them will achieve this. It also shows you trust them and are prepared to throw them in at the deep end.

The jobs you give them on their first day need to help them feel important. Therefore there are certain rules that apply:

- **Don't give them mundane jobs.**
- **Don't give them the worst jobs to do, such as filing or making tea.**
- **Give them something to do that is directly relevant to why they have been employed.**
- **Don't dump too heavy a workload on them on their first day.**
- **Give them things to do where they feel challenged but not snowed under.**
- **Make sure they are supervised.**

That should about do them for a first day. They will be exhausted but reassured, stretched but not overwhelmed. They will have met some of the people they will be working with and bonded with their buddy. They will have had a tour of the building and found out where all the really useful amenities are, such as the lavatories, canteen and coffee-making facilities. They will go home feeling satisfied and confident that they made the right choice.

And you can also go home knowing you've done a great job and that you too made the right choice.

DAY TWO

You've successfully done day one. So what do you have to do on day two? Well, you don't have to take any forms or information off them. And you get them to turn up at the same time as everyone else, and work a full day. No letting them go home early today. Apart from that, pretty much the same as yesterday. If everything was in place for day one, then day two should be a doddle for everyone concerned.

- ▶ They report to you.
- ▶ You hand them over to their buddy.
- ▶ They do some meaningful and useful work connected with their real job.
- ▶ You leave your door open all day for any questions that might arise.
- ▶ You monitor them at regular intervals to make sure they are doing fine.
- ▶ You get them to report to you at going home time.
- ▶ You get the buddy to report to you at going home time.

If everything was in place for day one, then day two should be a doddle for everyone concerned

NO COLLECTIONS

Make it a rule that a new beginner is immune from all office collections for the first month. Chances are they won't know the person for whom you are having a whip-round and couldn't care less if Betty is getting married, or Trevor is leaving to work his way round Australia. They also shouldn't have to sign get-well cards, chip in for birthday presents, or fork out for retirement presents. They do, however, have to contribute to any funds, such as a coffee fund or tea box.

for next time

Make sure all your checklists are ticked off this time so that you haven't forgotten anything. If anything crops up that we haven't covered, add it to your checklist. Monitor how this new beginner slots in and you'll get a good understanding for next time of what works and what doesn't. Watch out for any mistakes they make, and take action to stop them happening again. This might include getting lost, going to the wrong entrance, or failing to find reception.

Monitor how well your team takes to a new beginner and make a note of anything that needs improving on next time. Take notes of how well the buddy system works and how your choice of buddy turns out. This is also a good chance to monitor the buddy, especially if they are in line for increased responsibility or promotion. Think ahead to how your new beginner can be someone else's buddy next time. You can tell them this so they know the score and already feel trusted and ready to take on a task in the future.

Monitor how well your team takes to a new beginner and make a note of anything that needs improving on next time

4 different needs

People come in all shapes and sizes, with different levels of aptitude, experience, needs and abilities. Throughout this book we have assumed that your new beginner fits into some framework of your past experience. But there are occasions when we have to induct a new beginner who, for whatever reason, needs different priorities or alternative working procedures, or even different access to the building. The variety of different needs that people have is pretty big, more so than you might think at first. We are all aware of the needs of people with disabilities and those from ethnic minorities, but what about school leavers? Or ex-offenders? Women returning to full-time employment after having children? Expatriates? They all need to be thought about when it comes to induction programmes.

These are some of the people you might be expected to consider and plan for:

- ▶ people with disabilities
- ▶ people with ethnic differences
- ▶ part-timers
- ▶ shift workers
- ▶ long-distance workers
- ▶ professionals
- ▶ women returners
- ▶ older workers
- ▶ school leavers
- ▶ graduates
- ▶ managers
- ▶ expatriates
- ▶ transferees
- ▶ promotees
- ▶ people returning to work after long unemployment
- ▶ ex-offenders
- ▶ temps
- ▶ job sharers
- ▶ home workers.

We'll look at each of these individually, but quickly as I'm aware that precious seconds are slipping away.

There are occasions when we have to induct a new beginner who, for whatever reason, needs different priorities or alternative working procedures

Nowadays these people are usually referred to as 'people with different abilities'. They are not disabled but *differently* abled. As long as you think like this you should be able to plan an induction programme to suit their particular needs. If you think of them as disabled, they may seem helpless. If you think of them as differently abled, they seem capable, but in a different sort of way to you.

Don't make the mistake of assuming that 'disabled' means a wheelchair. It doesn't necessarily. Not all differently abled people are the same. They are as varied as any other group of workers. Epilepsy, cerebral palsy, partial sightedness, partial hearing and diabetes all fall into the category of differently abled.

You will need to be aware of any special emergency or first-aid treatment the person may need, for example in the case of epilepsy or insulin shock from diabetes. You must also be aware of access problems and what account has to be made of the person's differing abilities in the event of fire or evacuation of the building.

The best thing is to talk to the person concerned before taking any action. You will probably have found out a lot at interview stage.

thinking smart

SEEKING PROFESSIONAL ADVICE

If you need any further information, contact your local Job Centre and ask to talk to the Disablement Resettlement Officer. The Royal Association for Disabilities and Rehabilitation (0207 637 5400) can also give very useful advice.

According to research, people with different abilities often more than make up for any interference with their working practices by keeping better time, taking less time off for illness and sickness, and being more productive. Just concentrate on what they *can* do rather than what they *can't*.

PEOPLE WITH ETHNIC DIFFERENCES

Your job as team leader is to make sure that no new beginner is subjected to any racial harassment. But this should also include cultural, language, background, social and religious differences. People with ethnic differences need to be accepted into your team easily and effectively. This may mean briefing your team in advance. Differences may include special times of day for prayer, special diets,

The best thing is to talk to the person concerned before taking any action

or written instructions in a different language. All of these things may have to be done to facilitate a smooth and easy introduction into the team.

PART-TIMERS

Everything you do for full-time workers you should also do for part-time workers. They are no different – they just work fewer hours for you. Any induction should take place during their normal working hours – just as it would for a full-time worker – and not in their own time. They may need more thorough training or training more often, as the gaps between sessions may be longer and thus they may retain less information. As a consequence, you may have to extend their probationary period to take this into account.

SHIFT WORKERS

The same goes for shift workers: training should take place in their normal working hours, and they are entitled to a full and complete induction programme.

LONG-DISTANCE WORKERS

These workers have little contact with the office and can be hard to include in an induction programme. But include them you must. You have to engender a feeling of belonging to the company,

thinking smart

ETHNIC DIFFERENCES

If in doubt, contact the Race Relations Employment Advisory Service at your local Job Centre. Seek advice from someone else in the company who knows and understands the differences.

even if they work at considerable distance from it, such as oil-rig workers, sales representatives and travelling maintenance staff. They may need special induction training in reclaiming their expenses, reporting into the office, reporting in sick, queries and questions, acting on their own initiative, or making decisions. They may also need pairing up with a professional buddy for a while to make sure they are being trained fully in company procedures.

thinking smart

PHONE WORKERS

These can be regarded as long-distance workers, and the same provisions should be made to make sure they feel they belong and that they have any special procedures under their belt.

PROFESSIONALS

The biggest problem you're likely to come up against with inducting a professional is exactly that – they are professionals. They are already trained with a relevant qualification. They may be someone such as the company doctor. You know they can cure the sick – or at least alleviate the symptoms – so why on earth do you need to induct them? But they too need to know their way round, who to report to, how to get paid, what to do if things go wrong, the fire drills and emergency procedures, and where the canteen and the lavatories are. They too are human, and need to be reassured to feel that they are part of a team and are fitting in.

WOMEN RETURNERS

Ever tried bringing up children and running a home? Try it for a while and you'll find it needs a lot of skills and talents, such as budgeting, discipline, motivation, consistency, planning, decision making, supervisory skills, team building, inducting new beginners, maintenance and repair skills, diplomacy, negotiating skills and many, many more. Your biggest challenge with women returners is to imbue them with confidence. They have the skills but they need to realize they are valued and valid in the workplace. Once you are over the confidence hurdle, you can induct them as any other group of workers.

OLDER WORKERS

They may have become set in their ways. They may have seen it all. They may well have been 'doing this when you were still having your bottom wiped, kiddo.' But they do come with a wealth of experience that shouldn't be ignored or overlooked. Inducting an older worker may require a little more tact – giving them a buddy of a similar age rather than a young upstart will help – but you do inherit an awful lot if you do it right. They fear failure and rejection just like the rest of us, so work hard at reassuring them and don't patronize them or treat them as if they are old timers.

SCHOOL LEAVERS

People fresh from school have many obstacles to overcome including:

- being trained on outdated equipment
- having no work experience
- having a poor attention span due to never having had a lesson that lasted longer than an hour
- having poor self-motivation skills
- having little experience of working alongside equals of vastly differing ages
- working on their own
- being unused to work discipline

- ▶ having no experience of working conditions and rules
- ▶ having no experience of equipment
- ▶ being nervous and unconfident
- ▶ having no experience of safety and health regulations
- ▶ having little decision-making experience.

But they do bring with them enthusiasm, an ability to learn fast, keenness to try new challenges, youth, energy, vitality, life and no bad habits (except maybe chewing gum, being late and dressing in a weird and strange fashion). Get them young and you have fresh clay to mould. You will have to spoon-feed them information to begin with and mollycoddle them a bit. But they want to learn and haven't yet got out of the habit of it. They may well have had a part-time job or a newspaper round or a summer job, so they might not be quite as bad as you expect. They may have done a little work experience and understand what is required of them. You will need to be patient and considerate.

GRADUATES

Like the school leavers, graduates may have had no work experience; if they have only recently been to university or college, they may have very little in the way of work discipline. They have the potential

A KINDRED BUDDY

If your new beginner is a recent school leaver, give them a buddy who didn't leave school too long ago themselves. This way you establish an instant rapport. The new beginner will look up to the buddy, and the buddy has someone for whom they feel responsible, which makes them feel grown up themselves.

to take badly to time keeping, attending meetings and being there every day. They may also have specialized in a very narrow discipline, which means they may find it hard to branch out or to take risks. They may think that what they have been doing will automatically lead to immediate responsibility and real work and find the reality very different and quite hard to take. They may also have no practical skills.

But they do have knowledge, enthusiasm, youth, a remarkable ability to learn, and great reasoning powers. Be considerate with them and give them as much responsibility as they can manage and you can trust them with. The faster you bring them on, the better they will respond.

School leavers may have done a little work experience and understand what is required of them. You will need to be patient and considerate

MANAGERS

They may well be experienced in the job but they will still need inducting into your company's procedures and disciplines. They usually don't want inducting – and the rule is the higher the post the less they want it – but they do need to know basic information as we have outlined before. You might not need to give them a buddy – in fact they may be insulted by such an idea – but get them alongside another manager of equal status to show them the ropes. They may need to know more about the company's politics than about how to use the photocopier, but they still need initial help and advice. They also need to get on with real work as quickly as possible if they are to feel happy.

EXPATRIATES

Expatriates need time to adjust if this is their first employment since returning to the 'old country'. Customs and work practices will be different and people will treat them differently. They need sympathetic induction.

TRANSFEREES

This group of people is usually easier to induct because they already have a knowledge of company procedures. But this can cause problems if there

BRIEFING YOUR TEAM

Your team needs to be briefed in the sort of differences likely to be encountered when taking on an expatriate as a new beginner, such as how to treat different groups of workers, how to address superiors and juniors, how to cooperate in a multicultural workplace, travel, language and currency. Returning home after a long period living abroad can be a bit of a shock. The expat has an expectation of what they will find on their return and is often sadly disillusioned. They will need help to overcome this, and help with modern equipment, which may well be vastly different to what they have been using.

are discrepancies: the 'But we never did it like that in Durham' mentality can prevail. Transferees still need guidance on their new job, even if it is the same job as they were doing previously. They still need to learn new faces and names, know the layout of the building, and understand your routines and procedures. Transferees are often ignored on the basis that they should already know everything. They don't of course, and they need their own induction process just like any other group of workers.

Your team needs to be briefed in the sort of differences likely to be encountered when taking on an expatriate as a new beginner

PROMOTEES

The same goes for promotees as transferees – they often get overlooked, forgotten or ignored. You still need to train them in their new job. Failure to do so can be disastrous, as it gives them the right to take you to an industrial tribunal if you dismiss them for failing to reach the proper standards for the job.

Promoting within a company is financially sound, as you save on advertising and interview costs, but it does have drawbacks as sometimes the team member doesn't get treated with the respect their new job warrants. Your induction process will take care of this, just so long as you are aware of it.

PEOPLE RETURNING TO WORK AFTER LONG UNEMPLOYMENT

These workers need the same degree of induction process as any other group, but they may well need extra care in bolstering their confidence and guidance with modern working practices and procedures.

EX-OFFENDERS

You will have known at interview stage what their offence was. Once employed – and you have already made that decision – their future with the company should be based entirely on their current performance. They are being employed to do a job and the only thing relevant to how well they do that job is their current performance. Nothing else. You mustn't inform the team or make a fuss – they have a right to have their background kept confidential unless they themselves wish it to be disclosed. Treat them as a returning worker who hasn't worked for a while, in the same way as someone who has been unemployed, but also be aware that they may well have acquired new skills or training in prison. Don't treat them like school leavers.

Temps

They too need to know the layout of the building, your procedures, and how to relate to other people within the organization, and should be trained in the job they are there for. Temps are often very good at adapting and fit in quickly – it's in the nature of their vocation. Nevertheless, they should be shown what to do and where everything is. If they fail to meet your standards, it almost certainly isn't their fault and it's no good just sending them back and asking for another temp.

Job sharers

Don't give each job sharer half of an induction process. Give both equal treatment and a complete

training programme. You need to qualify with them what happens if one of them is on holiday or leaves. You need to know exactly how the job is split and what that entails. And you need to know exactly who is responsible for which aspects of the job. Inducting job sharers is not without its challenges, but as long as each is treated as an individual and given full training you shouldn't encounter too many problems.

HOME WORKERS

People working from home for a company still need to know the procedures and company policies. They still need inducting. If they have reason to visit the offices then they will need to know their way around. They may suffer from being isolated and not feeling part of a team. Regular checks are essential to make sure they are following the company guidelines for work. You can stay in touch with them via e-mail and telephone. They may need extra training in modern technology; they will be relying on it heavily and won't have the same back-up and support that an in-house employee would have.

thinking smart

HOME WORKERS NEED TO SOCIALIZE TOO

Home workers should be invited to department lunches, drinks after work, staff parties and all that sort of thing. They too need to socialize with other team members and it makes them feel as if they belong and that you care.

for next time

Be aware at interview stage which category of worker your intended candidate will fit into, and be prepared to adjust your induction programme accordingly. Obviously this won't influence your decision as you will want to employ the best person for the job anyway.

If you are in any doubt about how various groups should be inducted, such as disabled workers, ex-offenders or long-term unemployed people, then contact your local Job Centre for further advice.

Find out what your company policy is regarding such things as disabled access, job sharing, flexitime, temps, teleworkers and others working from home. This way you can tailor your induction package in advance and have a set of guidelines already laid down before the interview stage. To be prepared is smart thinking.

They too need to socialize with other team members and it makes them feel as if they belong and that you care

5 follow-up procedures

So, you've successfully got through the first day – or couple of days. Now what are you going to do with them? Your new beginner is settling in, making friends, and learning their new job. Seems like you can relax. No way. This is when you really need to be on your toes to stop apathy setting in and the new beginner getting overlooked in the hurly burly of everyday office life.

Your new beginner is a valuable resource that you have invested in heavily. To get a decent return on your investment you have to follow a four-point plan:

- You have to be *committed* to their development.
- You have to *plan* their future.
- You have to put your plan into *action*.
- You have to *judge* how effective your plan is.

You might like to remember this as the *committed plan of action is judged*.

Let's have a quick look at how this plan operates.

COMMITMENT

Unless you see team members as instantly replaceable, you have to be committed to them both as people and as a resource. They are a valuable tool in your job. Without them you can achieve very little. It makes sense to want them to be stretched, challenged, motivated, stimulated, encouraged and praised. You have to want the best for them as workers and as people. You have to take a genuine interest in them. You have to care.

As a team leader it is often easier to see team members as units of work rather than people with all that entails, such as having problems, making mistakes, getting it wrong, being unhelpful at times, feeling depressed, being late, having off days, shirking responsibility and generally behaving in an all-too-human way. But the more committed to them you are, both as a team and individually, the easier it is in fact to be realistic and accept them with all their faults. You set your expectations at a realistic level and work with what you've got. Slotting a new beginner into such a philosophy is easy because you don't expect them to be perfect. But if you are committed, you expect them to do their best and, with your help, to rise to the challenge, enjoy their

You set your expectations at a realistic level and work with what you've got

work and want to improve and get on. Your commitment to them is to treat them well and be the best team leader they've ever had.

Plan

Every new beginner, no matter how humble their first job, has the potential to reach the top; to take your job one day, and eventually go higher than that. Every new beginner is an embryonic company chairman or managing director. Their time with you is part of their first step along that route. Some will fall by the wayside but all of them must be given the opportunity to reach as high as they want. This is where your plan comes in. You must have a plan. Not just for the first day or the first week, but for the next year and beyond that. You must start this plan before they start their first day. You have to map out their future – with their cooperation of course. If they start as a clerk, you must be looking ahead to the time when they will be a senior accountant. If they start by making the tea, you must see them as a potential finance director.

Obviously you want them to do a specific job. That is what they were employed for. You need to:

- train them in the job
- encourage them to look ahead to their next position
- start their training for that position while still doing their original job.

This way you have an ongoing training programme. As soon as they get promoted, you start them off on their next step, the next position.

ACTION

Every day at work should be a training day. That's a simple rule. Every day there should be some challenges towards the next step in the new beginner's career. When you train them in their job, you will be explaining to them why that job is so important – how the cogs mesh together to make the bigger picture. You explain their vital role so they feel very much a part of the team. And you begin to explore how they can contribute more by knowing the next step.

This training has to be realistic and ongoing. You must work out your plan and stick to it. There will be times when training is the last thing you want to do but as team leader it really is important to bring new beginners on. Just doing the job should never be good enough. They must be encouraged to take on more responsibility, increase their workload, try new duties, and expand their horizons. Having a team is a bit like having children. You wouldn't expect children to remain static. They don't. They grow and learn, change and adapt. Team members are your children and as their work parent you have to bring them up by training them.

JUDGING

No training is effective unless you monitor and assess it. You have to have an ongoing evaluation programme where you regularly assess the performance of each and every individual in your team (see *Fast Thinking: Assessment*). You must also have a process to judge how effective your induction programme is, and a feedback programme to let the new beginner know how well they are doing.

In any of these four key stages, you must use your discretion as to how to implement them; all staff are different and all teams operate differently. You have to look at your needs and adjust your training accordingly. But every day is a training day. Now you can confidently go out and greet your new beginner.

for next time

Make sure you understand and implement the four-point plan – *the committed plan of action is judged*. Work out how each and every one of your new beginners can progress. Try to see where they will be in one, five and ten years' time. Make sure each new beginner is given:

- ▶ support
- ▶ encouragement
- ▶ guidance
- ▶ feedback.

Make sure the goals you set them are:

- ▶ fair
- ▶ specific
- ▶ measurable
- ▶ attainable
- ▶ realistic.

No training is effective unless you monitor and assess it. You have to have an ongoing evaluation programme

new beginner in an hour

If you really have left it this late there is only so much you can do. The first thing is to set an objective (see Chapter 1) and make sure you stick to it: to *induct the new beginner effectively and warmly*. Make sure reception know:

▶ **who is turning up**

▶ **what they are to do with them**

▶ **who is to be informed when they arrive.**

Make sure you go and greet the new beginner personally and that you know their name, which department they are working in, what their job is and who their direct supervisor is. If you haven't chosen a buddy for them, do so now (see page 39). Select someone of a similar age and with similar interests, and quickly go and ask them if they would very kindly agree to do you this favour at such short notice.

Run through the checklist on page 29 of what they should have brought with them, such as their P45, National Insurance details and bank account details.

Introduce them to the rest of the team – but especially those they will be working closely with. Introduce them to their buddy. Have a cup of coffee and promise never to leave it this late again.

new beginner in 15 minutes

Under normal circumstances, if you'd really left it this late, I'd advise you to reschedule. But this time you can't. Even as you read this your new beginner is driving in through the main gates. You have only 15 minutes before they present themselves at reception.

Grab a notebook and write down their name, the department they will be working in, and what job they are going to be doing.

Make a quick decision as to who is going to be their buddy, (see page 39) choosing someone of roughly their own age. Ask the buddy nicely if they would be prepared to take this on at such short notice.

You just have enough time now to make it to reception and greet your new beginner. If they are late don't, for heaven's sake, give them a hard time. You've cut it pretty fine yourself.

Under normal circumstances, if you'd really left it this late, I'd advise you to reschedule. But this time you can't